Grandma's Rhythm and Rhymes

By Faith D.S. Pearson

Illustrated by Carolyn Fletcher

THE LITTLE PIECES LIBRARY

Copyright © 2015 by Faith D.S. Pearson
All Rights Reserved
No part of this book may be reproduced in whole or
In part without permission.

Faith D.S. Pearson, Author
Carolyn Fletcher, Illustrator

ISBN - 13: 978 - 1547154746
ISBN - 10: 1547154748

DEDICATED
TO
MY GRANDSON ANDREW
MY INSPIRATION
AND
MY HUSBAND STAN
WHO MAKES POSSIBLE ALL THAT I DREAM

My thanks, too many to count, to Ron and to Marta for their skillful technical assistance; to BettyAnn for her perceptive and analytical eye; and to Julia, a special thank you for her on the mark insight.

Clap your hands and keep the time,

Tap to the rhythm of the rhyme!

CONTENTS

PLAYTIME

DISCOVERY

MI FAMILIA

ANIMALS, REPTILES, AND FISH

TREES, TREES, TREES

SHLOOFIN TSAT

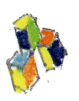

Wake up, wake up my little boy,
The sun is out today;
But if it rains, you still can play,
With blocks and trains and clay.

A sailboat is a special thing,
It glides across the water,
It sails upon long rivers and streams,
And in the bathtub shorter.

Good friend Drew has come for a visit,
　Something's behind his back, what is it?
It's a toy to share with good friend Sue,
　Does Sue have a toy that she'll share, too?

Dance around the kitchen table,
  Tap your feet upon the floor,
Beat the pans while you are able,
  'Til Mommy shouts, "NO MORE!"

Did you fall and hurt yourself?
　Don't worry little man,
Mom will kiss the scratched-up place
　And then you'll feel just grand.

1 2 3 4 5

UP

GROCERY  TURN

Discovery

RUN

WALK

 FORWARD DOWN

6 7 8 9 10

I like to dance,
I like to sing . . . . .

Though I am but one year old,
The sound of music lifts my soul.

Play the piano, strum the guitar,
Tap on the drum, dance like a star.

Ducks are yellow, bears are brown,
The sky is up, the earth is down;
A table's flat, a ball is round;
Eyes can see, and ears hear sound;

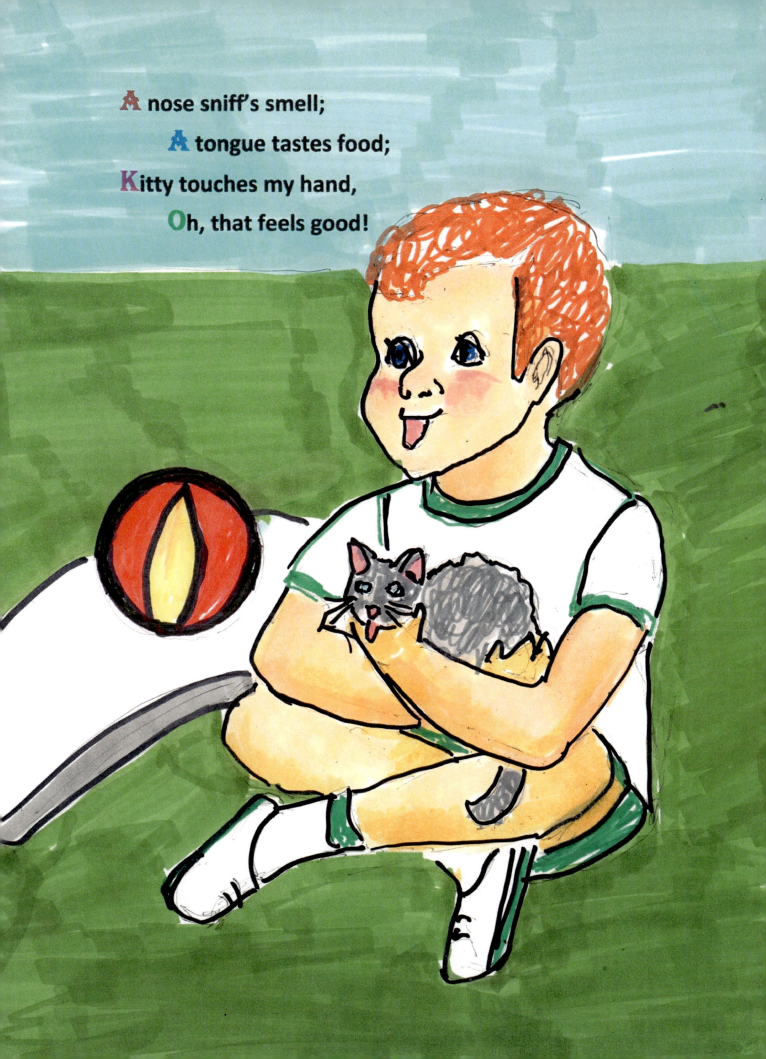

7. TAP QUICKLY

8. I CAN'T LAST

9. I GET UP

AND THEN I'VE REACHED

10.

NOW THAT I'VE FINISHED

I'LL START OVER AGAIN.

1 2 3 4 5 6 7 8 9 10

Mi Familia

Big sister, little brother
Throw the ball

Then hug each other.

Aunts and uncles are nice folk
  Who smile and hug and laugh,
But mom and dad are here to give
  Andrew food and bath.

Cheryl is a pretty girl,
   With eyes so green and slanty.
I think she is my cousin,
   Or an uncle or an auntie.

Great Grandma Flossie where have you been?
 I've been to the garden to pick some greens.
Great Grandma Flossie why'd you do that?
 So we'll have something to eat that won't make us fat.

 Turkey and taters,
  Carrots and corn,
 I've been eating well
  Since I was born.

Great aunts and great uncles don't come to call,
They're much too old to travel,
While great Aunt Lily is the greatest of all,
At knitting sweaters that don't unravel.

Marta is an aunt so dear
Who brings me books and likes to hear,
The things I do at home and play,
Then blows a kiss and drives away.

MINOR POLITICS

Mom's a Democrat, Dad's a Republican,
Well, what do you think of that!

When I'm big enough to vote,
Will I be Depublican or Remocrat?

My little doggy wags her tail,
Yet never smiles at me;
She licks my face and nuzzles my hand,
So she's happy, I can see.

Near the desert lived a boy
Who liked to search and wander,
He looked for geckos, lizards and snakes,
But of iguanas he was fonder.

The goldfish swam 'round and 'round his castle,
Then Curtis fed him too much bread.
The goldfish ate up all the crumbs,
And now he's very dead.

Scott's turtle left it's big glass bowl,
   And can't be found anywhere.
Scott looked under the bed
   And behind the door,
And hopes to find him by next year.

Alex was a fine young girl who liked to fly a 'copter
She'd fly above the trees all day
And nothing ever stopped 'er.

The mountains are a high class range,
With trees that reach toward heaven
Andrew climbed among the trees,
When he was six and seven.

Nanny, Nanny, come and see
    Me climbing up the sweet gum tree.
Nanny, Nanny, please don't frown,
    Just because I've tumbled down.

Runaway, hide, where can you be?
    Oh, I see you 'neath the apple tree.

Josh lost his cat, he broke his truck,
He hurt his thumb; what rotten luck!
Will he fuss and fret? Not he,
He'll go outside and climb a tree.

Grandma with glasses and Grandpa tall
Come to visit with gifts from the mall.

They sing to the little boy 'til he's fast asleep,
Turn out the light, from the room gently creep.

Where have they gone? They've gone away,
But they'll be back another day.

Don't wake up baby till her sleep has ended,
    Cause if you do she'll be offended.
She'll pout and cry and look so sour,
    For more than a minute, but less than an hour.

Hold him, rock him, in your arms keep,
    The little boy who is fast asleep.
He's gone to dreamland for a while,
    He's closed his eyes and rested his smile.
May all his dreams be happy ones,
    That last him till his sleep is done.

The day is over, you've had much fun,
   Now time for dreaming has begun.

Will you dream of dragons, ogres, or trolls,
 Or of Haley playing with baby dolls?
Will there be visions of earth, moon, and stars,
 Of bicycles, wagons, scooters, or cars?

Oh, sleepy time, please don't delay,
 Soon Andrew will be ready to start a new day!

THE END

Made in the USA
San Bernardino, CA
01 September 2018